Read for a Better World™

BUNNIES
A First Look

ANNA ANDERHAGEN

GRL Consultant, Diane Craig, Certified Literacy Specialist

Lerner Publications ◆ Minneapolis

Educator Toolbox

Reading books is a great way for kids to express what they're interested in. Before reading this title, ask the reader these questions:

What do you think this book is about? Look at the cover for clues.

What do you already know about bunnies?

What do you want to learn about bunnies?

Let's Read Together

Encourage the reader to use the pictures to understand the text.

Point out when the reader successfully sounds out a word.

Praise the reader for recognizing sight words such as *are* and *they*.

TABLE OF CONTENTS

Bunnies

Baby rabbits are called bunnies, kittens, or kits.

Bunnies have no fur when they are born. Their eyes and ears are closed.

Bunnies drink their mom's milk.
They drink once a day.

Most bunnies have brothers and sisters.

Do you have any brothers or sisters?

10

Some rabbits have fourteen or more bunnies at once!

While their mom is away, bunnies hide in the nest.

At about three weeks old, bunnies start to eat grass, hay, and veggies.

What do you like to eat?

Bunnies love to play.
They jump high and far.

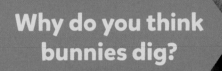

Why do you think bunnies dig?

When they are happy,
bunnies grind their teeth.
They like to dig.

17

Rabbits can live for ten years or more.

Bunnies jump for joy!

You Connect!

Have you ever seen a bunny?

What is something you like about bunnies?

What do you do when you are happy?

STEM Snapshot

Encourage students to think and ask questions like scientists. Ask the reader:

What is something you learned about bunnies?

What is something you noticed about bunnies in the pictures in this book?

What is something you still don't know about bunnies?

Photo Glossary

dig

hay

nest

veggies

Learn More

Geister-Jones, Sophie. *Rabbits*. Minneapolis: Pop!, 2020.

McDonald, Amy. *Rabbits*. Minneapolis: Bellwether Media, 2021.

Sikkens, Crystal. *The Life Cycle of a Rabbit*. New York: Crabtree Publishing Company, 2019.

Index

Photo Acknowledgments

The images in this book are used with the permission of: © kaew6566/iStockphoto, pp. 4–5; © Ilmar Idiyatullin/iStockphoto, pp. 6–7; © Taras Atamaniv/Shutterstock Images, pp. 8–9; © UNIKYLUCKK/Shutterstock Images, p. 10; © Anikakodydkova/Shutterstock Images, p. 11; © MidwestWilderness/iStockphoto, pp. 12–13, 23 (bottom left); © UNIKYLUCKK/Shutterstock Images, pp. 14–15, 23 (bottom right); © Voren1/iStockphoto, pp. 14, 23 (top right); © Rita_Kochmarjova/Shutterstock Images, p. 16; © Viktoria Szabo/Shutterstock Images, pp. 17, 23 (top left); © Sasiistock/iStockphoto, pp. 18–19; © Natthapon Muttabunnakarn/iStockphoto, p. 20.

Cover Photograph: © Smart Future/Adobe Stock

Design Elements: © Mighty Media, Inc.

Lerner Publications Company
An imprint of Lerner Publishing Group, Inc.
241 First Avenue North
Minneapolis, MN 55401 USA

For reading levels and more information, look up this title at www.lernerbooks.com.

Main body text set in Mikado a Medium.
Typeface provided by Hannes von Doehren.

Library of Congress Cataloging-in-Publication Data

Names: Anderhagen, Anna, author.
Title: Bunnies : a first look / Anna Anderhagen.
Description: Minneapolis : Lerner Publications, [2025] | Series: Read about baby animals (read for a better world) | Includes bibliographical references and index. | Audience: Ages 5–8 | Audience: Grades K–1 | Summary: "Did you know that bunnies grind their teeth when they are happy? Exciting photographs and engaging text help young readers learn about these adorable baby animals"—Provided by publisher.
Identifiers: LCCN 2023031855 (print) | LCCN 2023031856 (ebook) | ISBN 9798765626344 (library binding) | ISBN 9798765629468 (paperback) | ISBN 9798765636527 (epub)
Subjects: LCSH: Rabbits—Infancy—Juvenile literature.
Classification: LCC QL737.L32 A653 2025 (print) | LCC QL737.L32 (ebook) | DDC 599.32/139—dc23/eng/20231108

LC record available at https://lccn.loc.gov/2023031855
LC ebook record available at https://lccn.loc.gov/2023031856

Manufactured in the United States of America
1 - CG - 7/15/24